BLOOMS & DREAMS

BLOOMS & DREAMS

Cultivating Wellness, Generosity & a Connection to the Land

MISHA GILLINGHAM

GIBBS SMITH
TO ENRICH AND INSPIRE HUMANKIND

First Edition
26 25 24 23 22   5 4 3 2 1

Text and Photographs © 2022 Misha Gillingham
Photographs by: Fiona Margo: 3, top right; 5; 10, bottom; 14, top right and bottom left; 20; 21; 79
Alexis Gonzalez: 29; 30; 44; 65; 66; 70; 94; 100; 112; 116; 121; 135; 137; 164; 172; 175; 177; 180; 187; 194; 196

Published by
Gibbs Smith
P.O. Box 667
Layton, Utah 84041

1.800.835.4993 orders
www.gibbs-smith.com

Editor: Kenzie Quist
Designer: Ryan Thomann and Virginia Snow
Production Editor: Gleni Bartels
Production Manager: Felix Gregorio

Printed and bound in China
Gibbs Smith books are printed on either recycled, 100% post-consumer waste, FSC-certified papers or on paper produced from sustainable PEFC-certified forest/controlled wood source. Learn more at www.pefc.org.

Library of Congress Cataloging-in-Publication Data

Names: Gillingham, Misha, author.
Title: Blooms and dreams : cultivating wellness, generosity, and a connection to the land / Misha Gillingham.
Identifiers: LCCN 2021055623 | ISBN 9781423660200 (hardcover) | ISBN 9781423660217 (epub)
Subjects: LCSH: Gardens—Washington (State)—Bainbridge Island. | Farms, Small—Washington (State)—Bainbridge Island. | Evergreen Acres (Bainbridge Island, Wash.)
Classification: LCC SB451.34.W2 G55 2022 | DDC 635.09797--dc23/eng/20220224
LC record available at https://lccn.loc.gov/2021055623

FOR WILLOW, LIAM & MARIGOLD

TABLE OF CONTENTS

Introduction

When you imagine your dream life, do you picture someone bringing you gourmet snacks while you lounge in a cocktail dress by an infinity pool in the Maldives? Or do you picture your spouse bringing you a shovel so you can scoop alpaca poop while wearing sweatpants covered in goat hair? The latter is most certainly not what I had dreamed up for my future, and yet, here I am, happy as ever. To think I've actually chosen this poop-scooping life over the luxurious and glamorous world-traveler life sounds a bit crazy, I know. However, as I write this with a pandemic running rampant and so much political and digital madness happening all around us, I could not be more thrilled with our decision to leave our old lives behind. Now we are building a more purposeful, more fulfilling, and healthier lifestyle that allows us to lend a hand to others in need. Also . . . flowers. Loads and loads of flowers! But more on them in a bit.

Our big move from city life to farm life was initially fueled by the need to improve our family's physical wellness and mental health. Before we moved, I had cancer and one of our two daughters was diagnosed with a serious illness. My husband and I knew we needed a lifestyle change—in a big way. We purchased a quiet farm on Bainbridge Island in Washington, away from the hustle and bustle of Los Angeles, and immediately felt a wave of relief. After all these years of moving, traveling around, and not finding a place to fit in, it was as if we had finally found the missing "peace" of the puzzle—the place we were always meant to be.

I'm a former luxury travel writer and blogger. Originally from the Los Angeles area, I've spent most of my adult life living at a fast pace where I focused too much energy in all the wrong places. I actually thought "happiness" was a destination that you reached by getting on an airplane. In just a few years, I traveled to more than ninety different countries reviewing, photographing, and writing about the world's top luxury hotels. It was exciting, and, believe me, I do realize how incredibly lucky I was to have been able to experience all of that. But now I understand that alluring distractions and happiness are not the same thing.

I know it may seem like the dream job to many, but after a while, it stirred up a sort of emptiness inside me. Not only was I constantly lonely, exhausted, and unfulfilled, but also my experience of travel blogging went from being something I was passionate about to being a totally fake world that I wanted nothing to do with, a world that had lost its way. (In actuality, I think it may have been me that had lost my way.) It seemed that instead of using travel to authentically experience and share new cultures and places, it became a competition among bloggers to see who could get the best staged photo of themselves in an exotic setting. Of course, the same can be said about any niche on social media, but ultimately your experience will reflect your own state of mind, as well as the community you choose to surround yourself with.

I used to take photos in front of infinity pools in Africa, with massive platters of gourmet food, and elephants walking by. Now I take pictures with vegetables. But you know what? I grew these vegetables with my own two hands. I started them from seeds. I watered and cared for them. I amended and worked the soil they were planted in. I watched them grow—and now I get to feed hundreds of hungry people with them. I hadn't built those fancy hotels. I just showed up and took a picture. Maybe that's why the satisfaction of farm life is so much stronger. It has created a huge shift in my values: Instead of seeking out temporary, evanescent pleasures, I've been seeking out purpose and meaning. Farm life has brought this in abundance.

This place we are so lucky to call our home has inspired us to connect with nature as part of our daily routine. It serves as a home for

our rescued animals and provides us with a space where we can grow thousands of pounds of food to donate to local people in need. On top of that, I'm growing fields of flowers for cutting, and they speak to me perhaps more than anything else we grow. I get to witness their beauty on a daily basis, and they are such a delight to donate because they immediately put smiles on faces and brighten up homes.

There are so many fun ways to find joy from gardening and farming, and so many different types of gardens and farms. What follows is a very condensed version of how I started my farm and garden. I could write an entire book on this process (and I just might in the future), but through these pages I hope to inspire you to consider a life for yourself centered around wellness, giving, growing, and a connection with the land—be it a small potted dahlia plant or an entire farm.

—MISHA GILLINGHAM, 2021

Starting Our Farm

I never pictured myself in rubber boots, daydreaming of specialty flower bulbs and harvest baskets filled to the brim. Growing up in the Los Angeles area, I did not know a single person with a garden, let alone a farm. It was mostly city living. People had small lots with no land. I had no exposure to the farm lifestyle and no knowledge of anything farm related. But when my husband, Tom, and I were visiting Bainbridge Island on a business trip, we saw the real estate listing for the picturesque Evergreen Acres Farm, and it was love at first sight. There were three verdant pastures, expansive lawns, a pond, a sunny garden, a tennis court, and a handful of green-tin-roof buildings. Forests lined the perimeter and lush Pacific Northwest landscaping blanketed the grounds. A fanciful dream took hold in our minds, but this was not a dream we expected to become reality, since we lived in an entirely different state. It wasn't until three years later, when my husband needed to relocate due to work, that we decided to move to Washington from California. With our move, we were seeking a very different lifestyle—one that would promote healing after an extremely difficult time for our family. The stars aligned when we saw that Evergreen Acres was for sale again.

My husband and I purchased Evergreen Acres without looking at any other farm properties. There was no need to, because we knew this was the one and we felt ready to embark on a life-changing adventure. We had no prior farming experience and no specific plan in mind, but we still felt inexplicably drawn to the challenge. It was going to be a lot of work, a lot of planning, and above all, a labor of love.

It was August when my family and I moved in, and the previous owner had a delightful little garden growing. Alongside my daughters, Leila and Lili, I had the pleasure of collecting all of the treats that someone else had put in the labor to grow. We'd go over to the orchard to harvest various types of delicious apples, then over to the backyard trellis to pick some grapes and Adriatic figs, then over to the garden to grab some yellow Romano beans, rhubarb, tomatoes, and sweet corn. From this beginning, our very first farm tradition was born. We harvested veggies together and then cooked "garden soup" to enjoy outside by the firepit. Even though I had no prior gardening experience, and we hadn't planted this food ourselves, I was hopeful of what I might be able to do on my own. This wonderful new habit of gathering together to harvest, cook, and feast straight from the garden was a promise of something wonderful to come. I took notes from the previous owner's garden: I could see which things thrived and how to space them out, and I could see what needed to grow on a trellis versus directly in the ground. It was just what I needed to build the courage to set out on my own. Next thing I knew, I was passionately planning and then creating my future garden.

Our first few months on the farm were surreal. We spent our days working hard, transforming what was once someone's vacation property into our forever home. Warm summer evenings around the firepit while we soaked up pastel-painted skies over the Olympic Mountains became a ritual. I felt I could finally inhale a deep breath of clean, fresh air. Having mostly lived near big cities, my senses were now on a whole new journey. Lavender and fresh pine replaced the old familiar smell of car exhaust. Instead of busy streets, I feasted my eyes upon pastures, lush forests, and hydrangeas. Instead of hurried people, I watched sheep grazing leisurely. Instead of the tasteless week-old produce I bought at the grocery store, I enjoyed flavorful organic vegetables grown outside my door. I remember thinking, "Why, oh, why, did we wait so long for this life?"

At the same time, I'll admit I felt very intimidated. So many unfamiliar but necessary tasks were beckoning for my attention. My list included remodeling the main house and both guesthouses, planning a home addition, painting everything on the property from brown to black, building new fences, teaching myself how to garden, learning how to care for animals, building new shelters, adding landscaping, a chicken coop, a greenhouse, entertainment spaces, firepits, lighting, and on and on. I'm normally an impatient person who wants immediate results. Strangely, throughout this massive project I've felt calm, like a voice has been telling me, "Enjoy the journey. It'll all be even better than you ever could have imagined. Just be patient, take it one step at a time, and work your tail off to achieve your goals." It reminds me of the Mae West quote, "I never said it would be easy, I only said it would be worth it."

My learning curve has not been much of a curve at all. In fact, it feels more like a steep mountain that I will never summit—but I don't want to stop climbing. To get started, I watched numerous YouTube tutorials, read books, and scoured the Internet. After a few months, I slowly began making some progress. But the information out there is endless, and even after three years, I am still researching, reading, and learning something new every day. Of course, my family and I have made many mistakes along the way, like the time we failed to properly latch the sheep enclosure. We learned of our oversight at two in the morning, thanks to a call from the local police department saying our livestock had been spotted taking a stroll down Fletcher Bay Road, stopping occasionally to munch on a neighbor's landscaping. There's nothing quite like driving around in a John Deere Gator like Little Bo Peep in search of her flock during the middle of a rainy night. Lesson learned: second gate latch added. But as they say, mistakes are the best way to learn. Besides, the learning process brought about some hilarious memories (more on this in future chapters) as well as some rather special family bonding moments.

Speaking of farm animals, my plan was to start easy with chickens. As fate would have it, though, our very first step in creating our

dream farm was the acquisition of the aforementioned escapees—six Icelandic sheep already living in the pastures when we bought the property. It turned out they were food stock and destined to end up on a local restaurant menu. My daughters and I are lifelong vegetarians and animal lovers, and we had already named the cute woolly creatures. So there was no way we were sending Boo, Bear, Bull, Baby, Stix, and Cleo off to the butcher. We had a quick and friendly negotiation with the neighboring farmer who had been temporarily keeping

his flock in our pasture, and all six sheep received clemency. Next, we adopted five adorable baby goats from the Puget Sound Goat Rescue.

After that, Antonio, our alpaca, made his way over to us when a neighbor needed to find him a new home. Then, our third German shepherd puppy, Violet, joined our family because, why not? Funny enough, we ended up getting the chickens last. Today, we have over thirty-five resident animals here on the farm as pets—guests, really—and they bring us smiles just about every day.

However, when it comes to bringing on the smiles, as I've mentioned, I recently discovered that nothing makes me grin from the inside out like good old-fashioned homegrown flowers. A few months after we purchased the farm, my husband suggested we turn our front pasture into a flower field. He meant just sprinkling some wildflower seeds across it, but my imagination ran wild. I envisioned a dreamland full of dahlias, tulips, peonies, and more, all curated and coordinated to create a very special place. I didn't want to set it up like a typical flower farm, grown in massive rows to sell. The design and experience of this space mattered. I wanted a magical wonderland that my friends and family could escape to and get lost in, and that's exactly what I set out to create. But first, I spent an entire year planning and learning in my "practice garden."

Since the previous owner had a nice garden growing when we moved in, I was able to see what grew well in this zone, and I attempted to grow some of those same things. But I also just experimented with planting food and flowers that I liked, with the hope that they'd thrive. We are lucky here in zone 8b because our climate allows us to grow such a large variety of crops and blooms. I made many trips to our island nurseries to ask questions and get help with selecting plants. In the process of cultivating the garden, I experienced an incredible amount of joy and so much abundance. As a first-year gardener, this was completely unexpected. It was as if our property was under a fairy godmother's magic spell. Not only did everything grow, but things grew huge and plentiful, with minimal pests. There were humongous candy-striped beets, which were as sweet as they sound, dinnerplate dahlias twice the size of my head, and massive zucchini that grew faster than I could harvest them. Cosmos and zinnias sprung out of every nook and cranny, while Kentucky Wonder green beans, spaghetti squash, and scarlet runner vines went wild.

I felt the urge to share all of the delicious beauty we had been blessed with. Surely, all of this was not just here for our family to enjoy alone. The idea for a "giving garden" started to develop in my mind. Having recently shut down my travel business, I was in search of something to pour my heart and creativity into. I thought, "Why not share these wonderful garden treasures with our local community?" My family and I could donate our organic food and specialty flowers to people in need through our local food bank. This seemed like a fantastic way to spread the magic that our farm was producing so abundantly. So with the help of my daughters, husband, friends, and family, the Evergreen Acres Giving Garden was born, and it has been one of the most rewarding experiences of my life.

The Lay of the Land

Our farm is made up of 9.5 sunny acres and 2.5 forested acres. We have multiple gardens—the biggest of those are the main garden, the lavender garden, and the pond garden. Each space brings a different form of beauty and abundance. Many of these spaces are currently being renovated as we work to bring visual continuity to the farm. What follows is a quick tour of some of my favorite areas around the property, starting at the front and working our way around the farm.

FRONT PASTURE & BARN

The first thing you'll see when you enter our farm is our green-roofed black barn and our adorable woolly family members. You'll be formally introduced to them in the next chapter, but here are some photos of them modeling their barn and green pasture. I purposely put the garden right next to the front pasture so I could keep an eye on my babies, especially the newborns, while I'm working in the soil.

GIVING GARDEN

The garden, oh, the garden! It's the most beautiful form of self-care; it grows and nurtures the gardener in more ways than it does the plants. In this space, I have discovered so much more than what springs to life around me—I've discovered what springs to life *within* me. It's where I go to meet up with my best self. It's where I have found fulfillment, creativity, and peace of mind like never before. The Giving Garden gives full bellies, fresh air, beauty, and joy. It is truly the gift that keeps on giving.

GREENHOUSE

I waited three years for this, and it's finally
here: a greenhouse with a black frame,
stone stem wall, and black grout. This was
something I had been dreaming of since
we moved in. It has finally been completed
and I couldn't be happier to be able to grow
plants year-round and have a covered, shel-
tered oasis in the center of the garden where
I can relax or hold dinner parties. I can use
it to stargaze or even spend a night under
the moonlight. It's a place where I craft,
and sometimes where I sit to work on my
computer. It is not just a greenhouse; it's a
multipurpose structure that feels like it is
one with nature.

CHICKEN COOP

Every morning I spend time with our seven sweet hens. They sing to me while I collect their nutritious, organic, cruelty-free eggs. It's true—fresh eggs from healthy chickens do taste better. Our feathered ladies seem to be pretty happy with their black-cedar coop, especially Poppy, who always comes to greet me after her morning egg song. And French Fry, our Araucana, is especially proud of her pretty blue shells. These girls love to prance around their coop—styled out with annual planting beds, climbing vines, and a "chick-nic" table—taking dust baths any chance they get. The coop was designed by local architecture firm, Atelier Drome, alongside our chicken coop builder, Rob Campbell (from Campbell's Chicken Coop). I especially love the egg-collecting door where our girls lay their colorful offerings. There are access doors on all sides so we can keep it nice and clean.

GARDEN SHED & HARVEST STATION

I revived our junky, dusty storage shed from its sad state of Rip Van Winkle slumber into a nice cool sanctuary to relax in on a warm summer day. When the garden gets too hot and my back and hands have had enough, the shade of the She Shed beckons me inside to read a book or write in my journal. This is also a space I use to arrange and store flowers, as well as fresh food harvests, since it is guarded from the sun.

The harvest station is attached to the side of the garden shed, and it's a bit makeshift since we threw it together in the area where the old goat barn used to be. It's covered by the shed's roof overhang, so I decided to add shelves and store some of my frequently used supplies here. It's where I keep my aprons, harvest buckets, tools, and more. My husband built our washing and harvesting tables using leftover cedar from our raised beds, as well as leftover chicken wire from the coop.

POND GARDEN

Springtime turns the pond into my favorite slice of paradise on the farm. It's where the songbirds sing and the frogs gleefully croak their symphonies. Stepstones cross the water to cheerful Apricot Whirl daffodils and fluffy Ice Cream tulips, while the scents of Royal Lavender sweet peas and lilacs waltz through the air. This is the spot where I was recently seduced into my newest love affair—no, not with a bearded man, but with the beautiful bearded iris. It also happens to be the favorite play area of our three German shepherds, who swim and splash all day without a care in the world (demonstrated by their daily habit of trampling my flowers).

SPORTS ARENA & SUPPLY ROOMS

The previous farm owner turned what was then a riding arena into a sport court, which is used daily by our local community. When the pandemic hit in 2020, there was a lack of facilities for various youth activities such as tennis, ballet, and orchestra practice. We donated the use of the sport court to local residents because it offers cover from the rain but is still open to the outdoors, allowing for ample airflow. It is still used daily by our community, and we feel very lucky to be able to offer support in this way.

Along the inside of the arena we have four supply rooms, which hold the feed for our animals and supplies for our farm. I have dreams of turning this arena into an event space, but that's pretty far down on the list, so for now it'll stay a sports arena.

BOCCE BALL COURT

We take bocce ball seriously in our family. My husband and I have an ongoing bocce feud with both of my sisters and their husbands. Every time we all get together, we play bocce, sit around the firepit, and things get competitive. We love this area for entertaining and have future plans to add an outdoor kitchen and a pool.

SIDE PASTURES & SHEEP SHELTERS

Our Icelandic sheep live in the side pastures. The goats, alpacas, and
Babydoll sheep also spend some time in this space when it's time to
rotate pastures. Having three pastures is a necessity with all of these
animals, because we can rotate them, which is very important for
keeping parasites to a minimum and letting the pastures regrow.
The rams have already destroyed their new barn, which is now not
very photogenic but still does the job.

GUEST COTTAGE
& BUNKHOUSE

Remodeling our guest cottage was one of the first projects we tackled
when we moved to the farm. We wanted to brighten it up, soften the
color tones, and give it more of a farmhouse vibe. One of my favorite
things in the cottage is the custom painting of our baby sheep, Patches,
and her mama, Stix, painted by Lauren Spindle (laurenspindle.com).
Another one of my favorite things is the massive white cloud sofa. Once
you lay down, it's hard to get up. Netflix, anyone?

The bunkhouse is currently being renovated. It houses our home
offices on the first floor and a sweet bunk room on the top floor with
six beds. It's just perfect for our teenage girls' sleepover parties!

OUR HOME, SWEET HOME

As I write this, our home, sweet home is not looking as perky as the rest of our property. We've been planning and looking forward to a remodel since we first moved in, but for some reason, every time we are about to start, something prevents us from moving forward. So for now we are just sitting tight until the right time presents itself.

Our home's interior décor concept will be based around the garden. I want to bring the lines, patterns, and palette from nature into my home in an eclectic mix of industrial, rustic, and farmhouse styles. Who knows? Maybe a garden-themed home-décor book will follow.

FRUIT ORCHARD, GRAPE TRELLIS & LAVENDER FIELD

The fruit orchard sits right next to the garden, and it produces delectable plums, pears, apples, peaches, cherries, figs, and hazelnuts. However, since we don't use any chemicals or spray on our fruit trees, birds and deer do take their fair share of our harvests. We also have a bunch of grapes growing on a trellis outside of our bunkhouse. They taste like cotton candy, and the kids and I can't get enough of them in the late summer when they ripen. Our lavender is one of my favorite additions to the farm landscaping. The previous owners already had some planted here, and we decided to replicate its colorful look and aromatic scent throughout the farm.

Our Furry & Feathered Friends

They say dog owners are more likely to live longer than those who don't have dogs. So what does this mean for someone with three dogs, seven goats, eighteen sheep, four alpacas, and seven chickens? Immortality? Probably not, but our furry family members definitely bring us health and happiness (in addition to a whole lot of manure for the garden). People often ask me what purpose our animals serve on the farm since we don't raise them for dairy, meat, or wool. Our chickens do gift us eggs, but for the most part, we've found that our animals' presence is incredibly valuable in many other ways. They seem to lower our stress levels with their loving affection, nonstop entertainment, and silly shenanigans. That being said, they are a ton of work. Especially when one of them gets sick or a baby needs to be bottle-fed. The payoff is 100 percent worth it, but I don't want to give the impression that it's all butterflies and rainbows. It can be dirty, grueling, and sometimes even heartbreaking work.

GOATS

Often when I'm in a funk, I'll head out to the pasture—usually to the goats first because they're a guaranteed full smile. Kate and Delaney, our Saanen/Oberhasli girls, are always the first to greet me. Somehow under their soft, freckled pink noses, they always appear to be sporting a smile. London, our Saanen/Nubian will usually follow, and the first thing she does is try to grab a mouthful of my hair and swallow it down, only to gag it back up as I pull it back toward my scalp. (Hair secrets of a farm girl y'all—it's called a goat-throat deep conditioning.)

Liam was London's feisty twin brother and the leader of the pack. Sadly, we lost him last year to bloat, so I have dedicated this book to him (as well as to Marigold, a chicken we lost, and Willow, an alpaca who is no longer with us). I'm sure Liam is now in goat heaven, head-butting his dinner dates and stealing everyone else's snacks, as he always used to do. Rhys is our bearded silly billy—the only full-blood Saanen in the group. He's the one who just stands by my side no matter what I'm doing. This tactic was the well-calculated one that persuaded me to adopt him and his four buddies in the first place. We also have our two cranky-old-lady dwarf goats, Lulubelle and Daisy, who don't seem to like me very much. They always make me wrestle them to the ground when it's time for deworming and are always a struggle in one way or another—but the kind of struggle you welcome because it makes you laugh. Plus, how else would one learn to become a goat wrangler without a few poorly behaved goats?

GERMAN SHEPHERDS

There's nothing like having three restless German shepherds to keep your blood moving all day. Jojo joined our family first. She is our long-haired alpha female who behaves a bit like Eeyore, and quite possibly thinks she's a cat. She loves to be told she's a pretty princess. Then came Maverick, who has somehow acquired the nickname "Piggy Blockhead." He eats like a monster and ungracefully clonks his giant head into everyone he moves past. He's the sweetest snugglebear and loves his mama, but I'd never want to cross his path as a stranger. The

last addition to the shep-herd is Violet, our velvety black little lady. We were warned she was going to be "massive, easily ten pounds bigger than the others." Turns out her booty was the only thing that grew ten pounds bigger. The rest of her is small. "The Vi-Vi" as we call her, scares the socks off of anyone and everyone who dares to so much as walk past the farm, but little do they know, she's just a giant lover behind her sharp-toothed, loudmouthed façade.

ALPACAS

You might think our German shepherds would be the protectors of the livestock, but in fact, it is our "sweet" alpacas who wear that hat. I use the term "sweet" lightly because if you catch Sasha on a bad day she'll spit the entire contents of her stomach at you. But otherwise, they're quite beautiful creatures that are interesting to watch, and they take their job seriously. So far, no coyote or cougar has dared to come anywhere near our fur babies. We adopted Antonio, our male alpaca, with our two dwarf goats when their previous owner moved away. We were told poor Antonio had a skin infection when he was young and his face and legs are badly scarred. But he doesn't seem to let that hold him back. He is a fierce protector and the most social of our alpacas. Just recently, Willow and Antonio created Paco—the newest addition to our alpaca herd.

SHEEP

In chapter two, I told you how we rescued our six Icelandic sheep. When we made the deal to buy them, we were told that the males had all been castrated. Then this spring—six became fifteen! Our ewes each had multiple lambs. So they're definitely not castrated, and it's clearly time to put the ewes and rams in separate pastures. On a positive note, this did result in us getting to experience our first live farm births, which was so neat! It is incredible witnessing life being brought into this world.

I know moms aren't supposed to choose favorites, but if they could, Hokulea might hold that title. Hokulea is an ewe lamb, whose mother rejected her at birth. Luckily, with the help of my vet, we were able to get her some colostrum and nurse her to health. I bottle-fed Hokulea for two months, and in that time frame I became her mama. She cuddles me, plays games with me, and loves to be near me and vice versa. Honestly, she was born right in the middle of a really hectic and stressful time, and my first thought was that I could not physically handle bottle-feeding her through all hours of the night and day. I did it anyway, and the experience turned out to be full of comfort and love. Her presence has been a gift, and I have to laugh at myself for thinking it was going to be me taking care of her, when, in fact, it was the other way around.

Even though we don't use sheep wool ourselves (we donate it to those who do), most of our sheep are Icelandic, and they grow a massive layer each year that needs to be shorn for hygiene purposes and to prevent overheating in the summer. Shearing sheep has provided us with countless hilarious adventures. Catching large horned sheep in wide-open pastures is no small task, especially as a new farmer who hasn't a clue how to lasso. Did I mention they can jump about five feet off the ground? They should've come with a "Don't try this at home" label. But I can't complain too much; their poop is like gold for the garden, and luckily they create a lot of it.

Recently, three new sheep joined the family, including our beloved Babydoll, Zeb. He looks like a stoner teddy bear and loves to sport funky new hairdos which usually include some sort of hay or wood chips tangled up in his wool. Finally, our blind li'l ol' ladies, Thelma and Louise, arrived when their owner passed and they had nowhere to go. Now they'll live out their days in the green pastures at Evergreen Acres and we are so happy to have them.

CHICKENS

Last but not least, meet our feathery friends—our loving flock of egg-laying ladies have been such a pleasure to have on the farm. Their presence and cute little clucks and noises in the garden keep things feeling lively yet serene. Sometimes I just sit in the coop and watch them go about their daily routines: Sweet Pea, our Lavender Orpington, pecks around the ground for treats, while Hollyhock and Hellebore, our Black Copper Marans, sit in their nesting boxes laying their chocolate-colored eggs. Tigerlily, our shy Wyandotte, burrows into the dusty ground on the other side of the coop. Bluebell, our Blue Maran with fluffy feathered feet, is the largest of the bunch and she runs the show. She squawks at Emerald, our Black Australorp, who glows green in the sun, while French Fry, our Araucana, lays another baby blue egg.

The Practice Garden

I often receive messages asking, "How did you get started with gardening?" or "I want to start a garden but don't know where to start. Help!"

My simplest advice for anyone wanting to plant a garden is to first start with a "practice garden," like I did. Calling it a practice garden made me feel less accountable if things didn't work out. It also took away the pressure of having to make everything look perfect. You'll be able to learn a lot of the basics without having to worry too much about the way it looks. If something doesn't grow the way you had hoped it would, it's no big deal because your practice garden is for practicing and making mistakes. Don't beat yourself up if something doesn't germinate or if pests take down a crop. Just take notes and try to learn as much as possible.

GET TO KNOW YOUR GARDEN

In a practice garden you can learn which plants grow well in your zone versus which things may need some extra attention to get going. You'll learn how the light moves through your garden, how much water specific plants need, and what types of things to watch out for. You'll learn which pests you'll have to deal with and find a solution for. You'll learn what things might be helpful to add to the space, and what type of garden beds will be easiest for you to plant in, as well as how to move around and utilize the space.

Before investing a bunch of time and resources on my dream garden, I decided to spend a year practicing with a traditional organic in-ground planting plot. I needed to learn the basics of gardening and had a feeling it wouldn't be a very picturesque process. I also wasn't sure how much time I'd be able to devote to the project, so this gave me a way to figure that out before creating something too elaborate that I couldn't keep up with. Quite frankly, I wasn't even sure if I was going to like gardening or want to spend much time doing it. I knew that I loved harvesting and eating food from the garden, but was I going to enjoy the backbreaking workload that came along with those benefits?

START SLOW

There is so much to learn about gardening when you're just beginning. Entire books have been written on the topics of soil, compost, and seed starting alone. It can be so overwhelming. It was for me, so I decided to break things up into stages. First, I ordered some seed starting kits for a few types of veggies. I figured they'd come with instructions and I'd go from there. Then, at the recommendation of a neighbor, I ordered some organic compost from our local soil and compost store. (This was before we started making our own compost.) I had it delivered and mixed into the ground where I wanted to plant. After I started my seedling kits, I planted the rest of my seeds directly into the ground in rows, without doing any hardscaping or structural design. I needed to learn the basics and didn't want to complicate things by worrying about appearance or specific methods at this early stage. After that, the Internet quickly became my go-to source for gardening information—a quick search told me how to plant each item in detail.

TRY SOMETHING NEW

Once all of my vegetable seeds were sown, I thought I'd dabble a bit with flowers. I planted a row of cosmos seeds, two rows of dahlia tubers, a row of gladiolus bulbs, and a row of zinnia seeds. I also planted flowers in the water troughs the previous owners had used as their garden. The cosmos, dahlias, and gladioli sprouted up. The zinnias did not. Since I had an open space where the zinnias were supposed to be, and it was too late to start seeds, I transplanted some various flower seedlings from the nursery.

I had no idea what I was doing but thought it would probably make the most sense to plant the shorter plants in the front and the taller ones in the back. I also tried to make a nice display with the different colors. To my surprise, all of my flowers took off and bloomed like crazy. I never fertilized them and yet they kept on blooming and blooming. The immense beauty of what was developing in my practice garden caught me completely by surprise. This is when I realized some things: 1) Flowers grew well in my space and I could make them a larger part of the plan. 2) Flowers made me wildly happy, and I wanted to grow every single type I could get my hands on. 3) If I had not started with a practice garden, I would have designed my "dream garden" all wrong. 4) Gardening is a creative outlet in the most unique and satisfying of ways. This made me ecstatic about the future design project on the horizon.

REAP THE REWARDS

Watching the vegetables that I had planted sprout up and grow for the very first time was like winning a triathlon. I felt like I had accomplished so much. It was so exciting. I remember thinking to myself, "Oh my gosh, broccoli! I've grown Green Magic broccoli from seed. And wow, Adirondack Blue potatoes—they actually grew from their own dried out tubers. Butterhead lettuce—beautiful, crunchy, and delicious. Peas! I've sprouted Royal Snap peas on a twine trellis"— something I didn't even know existed the year prior.

Cutting my first bucketful of homegrown flowers made me smile bigger than a half moon. It sent pings of joy throughout my whole body. As someone who never had a green thumb, I could not believe I had grown these perfect flowers in such abundance.

The practice garden also helped me learn about the different methods to stake and trellis certain vegetables, such as tomatoes and pole beans, so that I could figure out which systems I liked the best. It taught me that I wanted a bigger workstation, better fencing, and much, much more space to play.

The developing scene was turning out to be a lot more picturesque than what I had imagined. I was really enjoying the process and added a few more containers and some string lights. By August things were looking pretty dreamy, and I was certain a crazy plant lady had possessed my mind. I was hooked, and that was that.

BED	PLANTINGS
1	celery, parsley bell peppers, hot peppers, carrots, tomatoes, cosmos, zinnias, Pansies, snapdragons
2	celery, parsley bell peppers, carrots, cucumbers sunflower, nasturtium, marigold, bach buttons
3	broccoli, dill, kale garlic, onions, chard, cucumbers sunflower, nasturtium, marigold, bach buttons
4	celery, lettuce, onions, cauliflower, carrots, cauliflower, cabbage, chard, cosmos, cucumbers
5	pole beans (flambo beans) on climber, carrots, cauliflower, cabbage, chard, cosmos, cucumbers
6	peas on trellis (sugar snap peas) bell peppers, eggplant, lettuce, parsley onion, potatoes, thyme, zinnias, cosmos
7	brussels Sprouts, potatoes, rosemary, celery, cilantro, sage, calendula, cosmos, pansies, zinnias
8	pole beans, broccoli, cabbage, kale, cauliflower, chard, calendula, bach buttons, echinacea, cosmos, nasturtium
9	tomatoes, carrots, onions, lettuce, beets, mint, bell peppers, pansies, petunias, snapdragons
10	edamame, kale, thyme, eggplant, calendula, beets, mint, bell peppers, pansies
11	peas, bush beans, cabbage, brussels sprouts, chard kale, lettuce, pansies, snapdragons, stock
12	broccoli, lettuce, carrots, pansies, calendula, bach buttons, snapdragons, cosmos
13	pole beans, beets, brussels sprouts, cauliflower, kale, pansies, pansies, nasturtium
14	lettuce, beets, bush beans, carrots, artichokes, onions, mint, bach buttons, pansies
15	onion, pepper, parsley, lettuce, red cabbage, chard, tomato, cucumber, pansies, snapdragons
16	pole beans, broccoli, rosemary, carrots, chard, lettuce, sunflowers, petunias
17	Cilantro, fava beans, beets, peppers, snapdragons, nasturtium, pansies, marigolds
18	Tomatoes, beets, peppers, snapdragons, nasturtium, pansies, marigolds
19	Sugar Snap Peas, beets, fava beans, artichokes, potatoes, petunias, nasturtium, bach buttons
20	Pole beans, bush beans, fava beans, artichokes, potatoes, petunias, nasturtium, bach buttons

Designing My Dream Garden

I designed and redesigned my garden about a hundred times. I had high hopes for it and wanted it to be as beautiful as it was in my dreams. After spending a year in my practice garden, I had learned a few things about myself and the way I wanted to use my space. For starters, I knew I wanted it to be larger—much larger. I loved every minute of the time I spent tending to the practice garden, and I wasn't afraid to go big. However, I do want to note that if I had just started with a giant garden first, I would have been extremely overwhelmed and shocked by the amount of work it takes. Slowly building up the work each year made it easier to determine my threshold. Another thing made apparent from the practice garden was that I wanted to plant my vegetables in raised beds, not in rows in the ground. The ground planting method was too much for my back and knees. I also wanted to plant a lot more flowers than I had originally planned, and I needed to design proper spaces for this.

THE VISION

My garden experiment had brought togetherness. It brought about a healthy family activity that all ages could enjoy, which helped me see how we'd want to utilize the garden as an entertaining space. I wanted to be able to have a place to sit and enjoy the garden, not just work in it. Whenever friends came over, the first thing they wanted to see was the garden. Once we went into the garden, we rarely ever made it into the house, so I wanted to add some seating areas and firepits.

To start the design process, I made a long list of everything I wanted in my dream garden: raised beds, flower fields, a chicken coop, a greenhouse, hanging lounge chairs, firepits, a fountain, and so much more. Did I add it all in the first year? Definitely not. But having an idea of what I wanted to add in the future let me plan spaces for the various things I wanted to eventually add in. In most designs, I appreciate symmetry and harmony and knew I wanted my garden to be as symmetrical as I could make it. I'm also very particular with my color palette. For hardscaping, I prefer mostly grays and blacks. For flowering plants, I'm drawn to shades of lavender, periwinkle, raspberry, dusty pink, deep plum, and apricot, and I choose my plants accordingly.

THE LOGISTICS

Drawing out my design was no simple task. I measured and remeasured my space, then I had to consider how the light moved through the area and make sure that no structure I was planning to build would cast shadows on my planting beds. I wanted my garden to face east, where it gets the most morning sunlight and allows me to look out over the animal pasture while I'm working, so that was a good starting point. With my focal point decided, I drew my raised beds around this area using landscape design stencils and graph paper. I drew up messy sketch after messy sketch, moving things like the chicken coop and greenhouse around from side to side. I also played with the ways I wanted the raised beds to frame the center area. Putting my ideas on paper made it a lot easier to visualize, even if I was the only one who could properly interpret my rough sketches.

Large structures, like the chicken coop, the greenhouse, and the central entertaining area, were all focal points I didn't want competing with one another. These were structures that were being added to an area that already had an existing garden shed and barn—that's quite a few structures within one area—and finding a way to keep them all as their own separate spaces was the biggest design challenge.

Photography has been a longtime hobby of mine, so when it came to placement of planting beds and structures, I imagined how it all would photograph from each angle. When I lined things up, I took a mental photo of them, and then I asked myself, "Does everything line up the way I want it to? Is anything blocking the view of the things I want to be able to see? Is anything a distraction? Is anything prohibiting the flow and movement of the space? Is there a clear focal point?"

Lo and behold, after about a hundred revisions, I settled on a layout. Now that I knew where I wanted to put the raised beds, ground beds, and other structures and features, my next step was to plan how I wanted to plant each bed and where I wanted to put each type of flower. There are so many different styles and themes for gardens that I had to create a mood board for myself in order to stay focused on the look I was going for, which is sort of a mix between a potager garden and a rustic farm cottage.

To achieve a cottage garden look, I added ground planting beds around the greenhouse, chicken coop, and right at the entrance to the garden. These were to be densely planted with many different types of flowers in many different colors. My plan was to layer the plants with the tallest in the back and the shortest in the front. In order to give the garden a cohesive look, I wanted to use repetition of certain plants and colors throughout the garden and wrote this into my plan. The raised beds were to be planted with vegetables as well as flowers—for pest control and for beauty. The size of our garden (roughly one acre) would allow us to grow far more vegetables than our family could ever eat and enough flowers to spread their joy far and wide. I loved the idea of being able to donate our bounty to our local community, and so we moved forward with that as a goal in mind.

THE SCIENCE

As part of the planning process, I did quite a bit of research on science-based companion planting and then made lists of what I wanted to plant in each bed. I numbered the beds and then combined plants that have similar watering, light, and soil requirements, as well as plants that have a good track record of growing together. Many plants attract the same types of pests, so I wanted to avoid planting those combinations. Additionally, some plants can stunt the growth of others around them and should not be planted together, and other plant combos can actually be beneficial for a multitude of reasons. For example, beans add nitrogen to the soil, which is great for plants that need a lot of nitrogen to grow, like most leafy greens or corn. Some plants can serve as a living mulch for others when planted closely together, and they can also deter pests and even improve flavor. In an organic garden, my belief is that the best way to keep pests to a minimum is to create a diverse little ecosystem. With many different beneficial plant pairings to choose from, I definitely recommend anyone wanting to start a garden do research and create a solid planting plan.

HARDSCAPING

When it came to hardscaping, I knew I wanted to use black as much as I could, because it seems less distracting to me and it blends in with the landscape. We used charred cedar to build our (mostly) 5 x 14-foot beds. Burning the wood sealed it, which helps it to last longer, and it also gave our beds a very unique look that includes the dark color that I wanted. At the base of each bed we put in metal screens,

similar to what we used on the chicken coop, to keep moles from digging up underneath the beds and eating the crops from below. As far as edging, we mostly used stones, as I like to use natural materials and we already had so much wood everywhere. The gray stones seemed like a nice contrast. Our ground within the garden is covered with decomposed granite and below it we laid down weed cloth.

THE EVER-EVOLVING GARDEN

For me, the garden is a never-ending work in progress, something that can be done in stages. After the practice garden, the next steps for my dream garden were to build the beds, lay the gravel, install the firepit areas, and build the chicken coop. The next year we added the greenhouse, decorative perennial borders, stepstones, pathways, pergolas, and outdoor rooms. I'm sure I'll continue to add to the garden each year, and each year I'll love it even more. The ever-evolving nature of home gardens is what makes them so fun. You can always improve or add to it—don't have to feel like you have to accomplish everything the first year.

6

The Giving Garden

The Giving Garden is my dream garden and an ever-evolving work in progress. It is made up of five outdoor rooms, seating areas, a fountain, firepits, pathways, arbors, trellises, raised beds, ground beds, and a whole lot of love. It is my sanctuary, the place where I can plunge my hands down into the soil and connect with my oldest friend, the earth. In the garden, I have discovered the antidote to the chaos and noise of daily life. Political debates, "news," and social media bickering are left at the upcycled-metal front gate—they're not allowed within the confines of the garden. Instead, I am present and focused on the task at hand. After all, I am responsible for cultivating and maintaining a whole lot of life between these hog-wire-and-cedar fences.

OUTDOOR ROOMS

Design-wise, I love the concept of the outdoor room: a growing and living seating area without the constraints of four walls or a ceiling. Since I like to entertain in the garden, I wanted to add as many out-door rooms as possible, without overcrowding the area. In the center courtyard, we put in two climbing vine–backed dining "rooms" where we can enjoy our morning tea or an evening dinner. The hanging bed-room, where a vine-covered trellis wall supports a swaying daybed, makes for the most divine place to lounge and read a book, while the swinging egg chairs create an intimate nook for conversation between friends. Each of these rooms is defined by an arbor, which provides some shade. The trellises support a living wall of climbing roses, scarlet runner beans, and clematis. The fifth outdoor room is defined by a stone floor, landscaping, and clematis climbing on the garden gate behind it. The bistro chess table is backed by roses and hydrangeas, while the larger table, also used for outdoor dining, is engulfed by peonies, hydrangeas, and snapdragons.

RAISED BEDS, GROUND BEDS & BORDER BEDS

Our raised beds are constructed of charred cedar. This idea came from Shou Sugi Ban, which is a Japanese method of preserving wood by burning it. We have twenty 5 x 14-foot beds that are 2.5 feet high, twelve 5 x 5-foot beds that are 2.5 feet high, and four corner beds around the center courtyard. These beds are mostly a mix of vegetables, herbs, and edible flowers. In the ground beds adjacent to and behind the chicken coop, I have two giant dahlia patches, with approximately 350 dahlia bushes, three large English rose beds, and four mixed flower beds for cutting. In the front of the garden, we have a large lavender bed surrounding our antique John Deere tractor. Across from it, we have a very large planting area for vegetables and fruits, such as corn, squash, and raspberries, that seem to do better in the ground versus in a raised bed.

And then there are two long border beds at the entry to the garden, with more surrounding the greenhouse and chicken coop. Border beds are my favorite beds to plant because I design them with a cottage-style look, mixing in a large variety of densely planted blooming flowers. Most of the border beds are full of perennials, apart from a few annuals that I like to plant along the front.

ARBORS & TRELLISES

Vertical elements in the garden are like icing on a cake. Not only do they add additional interest, but they can also serve as a screen planting, provide shade, and help define spaces. Our arbors are made of cedar posts with hog-wire trellises. Eventually, I'd like to have these completely covered in different varieties of climbing roses and clematis, which I have already planted, but roses and

clematis take a few years to really get going. For now, I have tucked in some scarlet runner beans, which is an annual flowering bean vine, to keep the arbors from looking bare while the roses and clematis grow in. As you can see, scarlet runner beans grow quickly and fill in very densely.

ENGLISH ROSE GARDEN

I can't believe I'm admitting this, but I was never a big fan of roses. That is, until I discovered David Austin roses, and then I became obsessed! This is year one for the rose garden. The plants are still babies, but boy, oh boy, they are producing an abundance of fragrant and decorative blooms! I can only imagine what the next few years will look like as they develop stronger roots and bigger roses. As you can imagine, this area smells like heaven. And the combo of colors— light apricot, peach-pink, and pastel purples—is a feast for the eyes.

PATHWAYS

In my opinion, pathways in a garden are so important, and are often overlooked. They're a critical design element that dictates how a person experiences a space. They direct people and their eyes to specific focal points. There are endless options of materials to use for pathways, but we used decomposed granite, Cowboy Coffee stepstones, and a river-stone edging. I would have preferred to use darker stepstones for more contrast, but we pulled these from another area on our property to help save on the budget.

LAVENDER PATCH
& ANTIQUE TRACTOR

An antique John Deere tractor was left on the property when we bought it. I don't know how many owners it has seen over the years, but we love it and wanted to put it on display. After positioning it in the center of a new planting bed, we decided to plant lavender all around it to add to the lavender we have growing on other parts of the property.

FOUNTAIN & FIREPITS

I was unable to find a preconstructed fountain with the rustic look I was going for in the garden. Many of them were too ornate and fancy, so we decided to put together our own, using the end of an old propane tank, sandblasted and rusted, as the bowl. Then we used a rustic old stone and an antique water pump as the faucet. The water trickles from the pump into the bowl, then over the edges into the lower pool, which is made of stones and grout. We love the way it turned out.

We wanted our garden to be a casual, comfortable place for guests to converse and relax, and there's just something about sitting around a fire that feels so natural. We built two firepits in the center of the garden because we like to be able to seat our extended family who come to visit, as well as any friends we entertain. The Adirondack chairs provide an inviting and laid-back atmosphere to be enjoyed by adults and kids alike. This is the prime evening spot for roasting marshmallows, enjoying a cup of tea, and taking it all in.

IRRIGATION

Our garden is a bit of a mixed bag when it comes to irrigation. We are still tooling around with what works. I'm not a big fan of having drip lines in my raised beds. I feel they get in the way and don't allow me to plant as densely as I'd like to. For this reason, we have micro sprinkler irrigation in our raised beds. However, we do have drip line irrigation in our border and flower beds because there is more room for them here and because flowers resent having water on their petals or foliage.

GARDEN DÉCOR & LIGHTING

I decided to place wind spinners and obelisks around the garden to make it more whimsical. String lights always seem to make outdoor spaces feel magical, so we installed those, but we've also placed pathway lighting along the sides of the raised beds as well as solar lighting along the fence panels. Other décor items we've added are planters and pots at the end of pathways as focal points, as well as at the entry to the garden. Our decorative, upcycled-metal entry gates were made by a local metal artist Bapatoms, and our signage was made by local artist Susan Roth, from Bainbridge Mercantile.

Flowers, Flowers & More Flowers— Year-Round

I feel lucky to be surrounded by flowers day in and day out. They are true gifts from nature, as they adorn gardens and kitchen tables, and they spark so much of my personal creativity. I use them to craft with friends, to brighten meals, to gift as arrangements, and to decorate my house.

It's not just the beautiful bloom that I love. The process of planting a flower from seed, nurturing it, and observing its life cycle is something everyone should try. It's like witnessing a thousand little miracles. I plant each flower seed with hope and a prayer. As the first seedling emerges from the soil, it sparks feelings of excitement. For me, this is followed by a new sense of responsibility as I try my best to care for it, hoping that it thrives. Then buds start to form on the foliage, and the anticipation sets in. Finally, the bloom bursts open and feelings of joy, accomplishment, and satisfaction are ignited. But also, I'm fascinated. The fact that the soil, water, and one tiny seed can grow into something so delightful is incredible and humbling at the same time. Then, as with all life-forms, it begins to fade and the petals slowly wilt. As it wanes it produces new seeds and new flowers bloom around it, offering up a hundred different metaphors for life. This beautiful and bittersweet process of life and death takes place before our very eyes over the course of a few months, over and over. It's emotional, and it teaches us some of life's best little secrets (which I'll share with you in How Gardening Has Changed My Life, page 185). I can't think of a better place to live than one that has a climate allowing for the growth of year-round flowers. What follows is how the fun unravels at Evergreen Acres.

JANUARY

At the very beginning of the year, in cold January, we are greeted by pansies, hellebores, and the first buds of anemones starting to wake up. This is also the time when I begin setting up the grow rooms in the garage and our new greenhouse to start my seeds. If there are any last-minute seed, tuber, or root orders that need to be placed, this is when I do it.

FEBRUARY

In February we usually get a week or two of snow on our little island, but the flowers only seem to bloom bigger and brighter once the snow melts. During this time, the crocus opens, hot pink peony shoots emerge from the soil, and the camellias awaken. In February, I start most of my indoor flower seeds under grow lights, which I will plant outside after the average last frost. In my case, this is early to mid-April. This is also the month I start preparing the garden beds and adding compost to the soil.

MARCH

March is exciting because the early daffodils begin to bloom, the anemones pop up in large numbers, and the scent of pastel-colored hyacinths fills the fresh spring air. Buds of blossoms form on fruit trees, and sunshine starts to breathe life back into the landscape. March is when I can finally scrounge up a variety of different flowers to make my first floral arrangement of the year. During this month, I spend a lot of time watering and watching over (and talking to) seedlings in the grow room. If I am planting any spring-planted flowers from bulbs, corms, or roots, which is faster than starting certain types of flowers from seed, this is usually when I do it. For example, you can grow new peony plants from their established roots, gladioli and lilies from their bulbs, and ranunculus and anemones from their corms. They can all be planted in early spring, even though they do best when planted in fall around here.

APRIL

April explodes with color every year. The longer and warmer days rouse the blossoming pink plum trees that line the front of our farm. Then come the azaleas, more daffodils, Muscari, and then, finally, what I wait for all winter: the tulips! April on the farm is truly magical. Everything transforms into a blooming, blossoming, flowering paradise. So many different narcissus flowers fill the area around the pond, emitting a blissful aroma that stems from shades of apricot, cream chiffon, and buttery light yellow. Tulips in all shapes and sizes span every color of the rainbow, and the arrangements I put together are extra fun. I always think the pastel-colored blooms make the farm look like it could be the Easter Bunny's hideout. April is also when I plant my well-nursed seedlings outside and when my dahlia tubers go in the ground. It's the month where the vision and design I've been planning starts to take form.

MAY

May brings yet even more tulips, lilacs, allium, irises, lupine, ranunculus, clematis, cherry blossoms, calendulas, roses, and so much more. The vibrant pink dogwood trees bloom over a sea of blue lobelia, and the greens of the garden appear even greener. The juvenile plants begin to fill in, reaching up for the sun, and the colors and light beaming through the farm look ethereal.

JUNE

June is a showstopper month, highlighted by my beloved peonies, hydrangeas, delphinium, larkspur, roses, calendulas, poppies, hollyhocks, and more bearded irises. Heck, even the artichokes bloom. My arrangements are full and fragrant.

JULY

We grow a lot of lavender on our farm, and in July it is at its peak! It is joined by gladioli, snapdragons, stock, lilies, foxgloves, more roses, and my long-awaited dahlias! It's also when the first cosmos and zinnias appear. In July, all of the plants really start moving, filling in very quickly. Fruit appears in the orchard, zucchini begins to flower, and an abundance of delicious garden food is ready for harvest. July is the month where I start most of my fall garden seedlings.

AUGUST

The warmth of August brings an explosion of sunflowers, marigolds, lilies, dahlias, Strawberry Sundae hydrangeas, and little bits of aster. August is my favorite month on the farm, because so much is in full bloom. It's a flower-cutting paradise, and getting to put together arrangements with what I grow from seeds is spectacular. This is the month where I start clearing out some of the spent veggies and blooms to make room for fall garden planting. August is also when I place the majority of my fall bulb orders; though, as specialty flowers become more and more popular, I have to order further in advance each year or things are sold out.

SEPTEMBER

Fall starts to creep in during September as the gorgeous periwinkle and pink asters bloom. Celosia and amaranth are nice and full, the roses are still going strong, and the dahlias are in full bloom, if you can believe it. In early September I plant my fall seedlings outdoors. I want them to get some warmth before the cooler temps set in.

OCTOBER

October's chill brings back the pansies and violas, which prefer cooler temperatures. It also makes a nice environment for black-eyed Susans, chrysanthemum, and more asters, which make for perfect fall arrangements. Late October is typically when I say goodbye to the bulk of the dahlias, but it's also when I start planting fall bulbs in the ground in anticipation of next year's spring explosion—things like tulips, anemones, irises, and narcissi.

NOVEMBER

We typically get hit by our first hard frost in November, and many things turn to brown. Most of the work in the garden entails pulling the remnants of the spent blooms out of the garden for flower cleanup, as well as seed saving. I also sneak in more fall bulbs all around the farm.

DECEMBER

Finally, in December, while most of the flowers rest, I rest as well. December is my month off from gardening. But I can't stay away for too long! I typically spend December getting plans started for next year's garden. It is also when I do the bulk of my spring seed and tuber ordering, along with anything I need for seed starting. Because there is less work around the farm in December, I spend more time cooking, and I love to use the pansies and violas as a garnish. I know that January is right around the corner, and everything is about to start again, so I take this time to slow down and enjoy.

Home Garden Favorites

I t's not easy to pick favorites, but it's a question I am asked quite often. In this chapter, I will share some of my favorite varieties of flowers and vegetables that we grow here at Evergreen Acres, in the order by which they bloom or ripen.

PANSIES & VIOLAS

I love pansies and violas because they bloom over the winter in my zone, and in a Pacific Northwest winter, any and all color is welcome. They are also edible and make a fun garnish for desserts and anything baked! My favorite types are almost all that come in shades of periwinkle, blue, and purple:

Celestial Blue
Chalon Supreme
Delta Marina

Matrix Midnight Glow
Ultima Morpho

ANEMONES

Anemones, also known as windflowers, are one of the first flowers to bloom here in late winter, bringing with them smiles and hope for the spring. Their timing and their neat-looking, ball-like centers make them a favorite. Here are a few types of anemones that I enjoy growing:

Anemone Lord Lieutenant
De Caen Blue

De Caen White

NARCISSI

I love narcissi (daffodils) because they're one of the first flowers to bloom in early spring, breathing so much life into my soul. There are so many different varieties, mostly with colors of butter yellow, apricot, and white, which add contrast and excitement to the early spring landscape. They also bring a heavenly scent to the entire garden. These are a few of my favorites:

Apricot Whirl
Extravaganza
Ice King
Peach Cobbler

Precocious
Replete
Sunny Girlfriend

CANDY-STRIPED & GOLDEN BEETS

Mixing these two varieties together in beet salads or other dishes is a feast for the eyes as well as the belly. Candy-striped beets are really called Chioggia beets, and when you slice them, they have a wonderful pink-and-white—you guessed it—candy-striped pattern on the inside. Golden beets are yellow-orange on the inside and have a delicious, sweet taste to them as well.

TULIPS

There are so many reasons why I love tulips. For starters, they're extremely easy to grow. You just pop the bulbs into the ground in the fall, and then, come spring, you have long-lasting colorful blooms springing up while most other flowers haven't even germinated yet. For some reason, I am most drawn to tulips in shades of orange, which is a bit strange considering I usually avoid orange shades with other types of flowers. What follows are my favorites:

Blue Wow
Brownie
Copper Image
Danceline
Ice Cream
La Vie

Orange Princess
Pink Star
Rasta Parrot
Sensual Touch
Valdivia
Victoria's Secret

PEONIES

I don't think I'm alone in my love for peonies. After all, they're the fluffiest florals in the bunch and come in so many different shades and shapes. My favorite types so far are these:

Bowl of Beauty

Coral Charm

Coral Sunset

Raspberry Sundae

Shirley Temple

PURPLE & GREEN CAULIFLOWER

I'm a big fan of unique vegetables, especially brightly colored ones. As a vegetarian, cauliflower makes its way into a lot of my recipes—from cauliflower "hot wings" to cauliflower "mashed potatoes." The fun lavender-colored Veronica cauliflower brings an element of excitement to my culinary creations and the kids love it. We also love the kaleidoscopic patterns of the Romanesco cauliflower Minaret.

CLEMATIS

Clematis is a climbing flowering vine with many different types of unique flowers. I have twenty different varieties of clematis in my garden. Something to note is that it often takes a few years to get established. Right now, I have one of my favorite types, Josephine, climbing up the side of our chicken coop. All the others have been planted around our trellised arbors and we will see a lot more of them next year once they are more mature.

ALLIUM GLOBEMASTER

Lavender is already one of my favorite flower colors, so when it takes form as a giant whimsical ball, it is sure to make my favorites list. Standing at about three feet tall, they make the perfect addition to cottage-style border plantings, or they can make a statement on their own when planted in mass.

RANUNCULUS

Ranunculus are spring bloomers that make their debut around the time the tulips are finished. Many people confuse ranunculi for roses, but they're an entirely different flower, though equally ruffly. My favorites are these:

Barby

Champagne

Juliette

Marshmallow

Salmon

BEARDED IRISES

To me, the bearded iris is such a luxurious and special flower. They are one of my absolute favorites for their intoxicating scent, unique shape, and giant ruffled petals. Bearded irises are not "cut and come again," meaning, with the exception of a few fall reblooming types, once you cut the bloom, they are done until next year. This makes them even more special. I couldn't even begin to choose a favorite type because they are all so unique and fabulous, but suffice to say, you can't go wrong with any type of bearded iris.

SNAPDRAGONS

I never knew how much I loved snapdragons until I grew Madame Butterfly Bronze. It bloomed so vibrantly and made such a statement in the garden. This led me to experiment with more varieties and colors. Here are some of my favorites:

Chantilly Light Salmon   Madame Butterfly Bronze
Costa Summer Lavender   Madame Butterfly Red

ROSES

I previously mentioned that I was never a huge fan of roses. However, after my first year of growing them, they won me over completely. David Austin roses are my favorites because of their unique, delicate structures. I love the following varieties:

Boscobel

Carding Mill

Olivia Rose Austin

Queen of Sweden

GOLDEN YELLOW ZUCCHINI

Zucchini seems to grow more abundantly in this area than anything else I've seen. If not harvested early, they can get massive. Because of this, I've had to experiment with many different recipes—zucchini bread, zucchini soup, zucchini noodles, stuffed zucchini boats, and more. Our yellow zucchini just seem to be more tender and tastier than other varieties I've tried. I never used to be a big fan of zucchini, but now that I know how to cook it in many different ways, it has become a family favorite.

SUYO LONG ASIAN CUCUMBERS

These curly, ribbed cucumbers are covered in a bunch of tiny spikes and are so crunchy, fresh, and sweet. I love growing them! I get to harvest so many from one plant, and they stay fresh for quite a while after bringing them inside. They make the perfect healthy snack on a hot summer day. I also infuse my water with them and use them in salads and numerous other dishes.

ZINNIAS

Zinnias are such a great flower for cutting gardens (gardens full of flowers grown for the sole purpose of cutting and arranging them into bouquets). They bloom for a long time and last forever in a vase. Plus, they're so easy to grow and come in such a large variety of colors. I'm really drawn to zinnias in shades of peach and pink. Cupcake Pink and Zinderella Peach are my two favorite varieties, and, as the name suggests, they remind me of a bunch of little cupcakes with their puffy centers.

DAHLIAS

Dahlias are the gift that keep on giving. They have a long blooming period, and the more you cut them for your arrangements, the more they bloom. Then, each year the tubers multiply and you can separate them to get even more dahlia plants the following year. This makes for one of the best cut flowers ever in my opinion. The return on investment is huge! Plus, dahlias come in just about any size, shape, and color you can imagine, which is why I have more favorite types listed here than with most other flowers. I tend to be the most drawn to the anemone flowering dahlias that look like powder puffs, but I also love dahlia balls and a few other uniquely shaped varieties. Here are my some of my top picks:

Blue Bayou
Bon Odori
Break Out
Caribbean Fantasy
Cornel Bronze
Josie
Labyrinth
Mambo

Natalie G
Platinum Blonde
Polka
Richard's Fortune
Sweet Love
Sweet Nathalie
Wizard of Oz

SCARLET RUNNER BEANS

The vines from scarlet runner beans grow like crazy and can easily cover any trellis or arch in the garden in just a few months. They have beautiful little crimson flowers that turn into large bean pods. But what's inside the bean pods is the best part—giant pink-and-purple beans that look like little galaxies. I call them "magic beans," and they make a tasty and hearty meal when cooked. Plus, you can dry these out and save them to eat at a later date.

HYDRANGEAS

Many varieties of hydrangeas grow well in partial shade, which is why the previous owner of our farm planted a bunch throughout our landscaping. I've added a lot more because I'm a big fan of the color palettes you can create with them. Hydrangeas grow mainly in shades of periwinkle, lavender, baby blue, cream white, and many shades of pink. Some even grow in a unique green apple color. I'm especially fond of how the colors of hydrangeas can change over time. For example, some will start out bright blue and then will fade to lavender as they go through their life cycle. Some of my favorite types are Nikko Blue and Strawberry Sundae.

POPPIES

Growing up in California, whenever I heard the term "poppy" I pictured the bright orange short-stemmed poppies that sprouted up through the ground wherever they could. I had no idea poppies could be long-stemmed, giant-blooming flowers of every color. They come in such a wide variety of shapes: Some look like fluffy peonies, some like pom-poms, and some that remind me of flames from a fire. In the zone where I live, poppies bloom only for a short period—in the late spring to early summer—but they're so worth it. Some of my favorites are:

Amazing Grey   Lilac Pompom
Iceland   Shirley

COSMOS

In my experience, cosmos are some of the easiest flowers to grow. A few varieties, which grow best in the ground, can get really tall, whereas others thrive nicely when mixed in with vegetables in raised beds. Some of my favorites are Cupcake and Double Click cosmos.

ASTERS

Aster is great because it blooms in the fall, long after most of my other flowers have come and gone. I love the frilly pink and purple varieties such as those in the Giants of California Mix, as well as the Ostrich Feather Mix.

GLADIOLI

I often hear people say that they don't care for gladioli due to their association with funerals, however, I think gladioli are absolute treasures in the garden. I find the colorful ones to be quite cheery and glorious. My favorites are Green Star and the Rainbow Mix, which are far from somber.

Donating Our Bounty

During trying times, the garden brings solace. When it seems everything is working to divide us, we can find common ground (pun intended) in our gardens. The Giving Garden requires us to work together for the greater good. I believe society needs more activities and initiatives that bring people together. Being able to share the gifts of the garden is healing, like a remedy to chaos, bringing meaning, satisfaction, and community back to our little world.

I like to think there is a reason we have been blessed with this farm, with such wonderful soil and so few pests, where everything grows so well. I feel we have this land because we are supposed to do good things with it.

Being able to spend time working toward charitable causes is a privilege, and something I am very grateful for. It is because of my husband's hard work and ability to support our family that I am able to devote my time to running the farm, cultivating the garden, and sharing what I love with our community and with the world through this book and social media (@farmluxe on Instagram).

Some say that charitable work should be done and not talked about. While anonymous giving has its place, I have found that sharing openly only encourages more giving. In fact, I never would have found out about the local food bank if our neighbors hadn't shared that they donated. Being vocal about the good you do in the world and the excitement you feel about it inevitably spreads joy and inspires others to do it too. My hope with this chapter is to share the ways we grow and give in order to inspire others. Let's build community together and take care of one another, which adds meaning and purpose to all our lives. It's a win-win for everyone.

WHAT WE DONATE

After our first full year on the farm, when my dream garden started to take form, I knew I would be able to grow far more than what we needed for our family, but being in the business of selling food was not something I was interested in. I had been searching for ways to give back, and donating the food seemed like a perfect fit. Once I decided this was what I wanted to do, I forged full steam ahead, and each year since, we've been able to donate about two thousand pounds of fresh organic produce grown in our garden. Most of it goes to our community food bank here on the island, and some goes out to other food banks in our county. Once a week we start early in the morning and do a giant harvest, collecting, washing, and crating everything that's ready to eat. From our garden we are able to donate large amounts of beets, carrots, greens, cauliflower, zucchini, cabbage, broccoli, green beans, tomatoes, cucumbers, herbs, and more. We also donate the fruit that grows in our orchard—apples, pears, peaches, and plums.

The same year we started the Giving Garden, my love of flowers exploded, and I decided we needed to donate flowers too, because they bring so much life. Some of these flowers go to the food bank with our weekly food harvests, but many others get donated to local events like fundraisers, memorials, and weddings.

As I mentioned, our farm has a large covered arena and sport court, which is in use (around the clock and throughout the year) by our community. We donate 100 percent of the use of this facility to youth tennis lessons, dance performances, youth orchestra, school recess time, and more. The children (and some adults!) really seem to enjoy watching the animals in the pasture across from the arena. We feel very fortunate to have such a wonderful covered area and feel it is our duty to share this space with our community.

Lastly, we donated the income generated from my garden show, farmluxe.tv to Helpline House, the Bainbridge Island food bank. We plan to do the same with the profits generated from this book.

I can't say it enough: I consider it a huge privilege to be able to dedicate my time and resources to these charitable causes.

WHY WE DONATE

Evergreen Acres overflows with abundance, and we feel called to share this bounty and the joy that comes along with it.

Giving flowers is like gifting a tangible piece of delight. Flowers are truly presents from nature that have long-term positive effects on our moods and well-being. Whether it's a small bouquet of Peppermint Stick zinnias or a complex towering arrangement of Blue Wow tulips, flowers have the unique ability to make us stop and appreciate nature's artistry. They create intimate connections between the giver and the receiver. We love to spread this cheer and all of the positive benefits that come with it.

We also donate homegrown fruits and veggies to encourage good health for everyone. I believe that fresh vegetables should be included in all of our meals and personally make them my main ingredient. Growing up, my family did not have the budget for loads of fresh, organic produce, and, in my opinion, nutritious fresh vegetables and quality ingredients should be accessible to everyone, regardless of their income. I'd like to help make this a reality in our community. My wish is to see more growers in all communities sharing the gifts of beautiful blooms and homegrown garden goodness.

YOU CAN DONATE!

Giving feels good. When we give to others, we are given a sense of purpose and fulfillment, as we work to foster a strong community. Working with friends and family to give to others strengthens bonds and relationships.

Many people want to do something to help others but don't know where to start, or they might not be sure what they have to give. There are so many ways you can help. Donating flowers puts immediate smiles on faces, and donating food fills tummies. Both are necessary and useful to improve everyone's quality of life. Growing food or flowers is a wonderful place to start because it gives you something tangible to share—something you've grown with love. You can donate your bounty to local food banks, senior living homes, hospitals, churches, or wherever you feel called to give. It doesn't have to be a massive amount; it can just be whatever is comfortable for you. Maybe that's a few bouquets a year, or maybe it's two hundred of them. It could be a small basket of food or large crates full of harvests. There is no such thing as a donation too small. And if you don't have the ability to grow, there are other ways you can give, like donating your time to help harvest or volunteering at a food bank. Look for ways to support and strengthen the community around you. I promise it will be worth it.

How Gardening Has Changed My Life

The garden has taught life lessons, given useful botanical knowledge, and provided me with countless therapy sessions, a creative outlet, and relationship-building activities to do with friends and family. It has brought me peace, confidence, resilience, purpose, meaning, and an inner joy that doesn't seem to fade, no matter what is happening in the world. It has helped me rid my life of bad habits and offered daily opportunities to connect with nature. I am forever grateful for the gifts of my garden.

GARDENING GROWS COMMUNITY

I have never experienced a community as supportive, friendly, and eager to help as the gardening community. I have met the most genuine and kind people who are excited to share their knowledge. When I first moved to Bainbridge Island, a shared love of gardening is what connected me to the people who would soon become my closest friends here. We have days where we get together and just work in the garden, harvest for the food bank, do garden crafts, arrange flowers, or cook with edible flowers. To build more community, I am currently planning various workshops open to anyone who has an interest in gardening.

MORE WISDOM EQUALS BETTER CHOICES

It has been eye-opening to learn about the very thing that sustains us all every single day—food. If grocery stores disappeared tomorrow, much of the world would not know the first thing about growing their own food. And it's not just about the food—it's also about the makeup of soil that it grows in, and the fascinating microorganisms within it that all work together to keep our earth and its creatures healthy. Once I started growing my own food and flowers, I began to look at everything differently. When I eat the food and cut the flowers that I have grown, I know how fresh they are. I know where they came from, how much love and effort was put into their life cycle, and most importantly, what types of substances have been used on them. I don't know what's in the soil that grows the veggies I buy at the grocery store. I don't know when they were harvested or how long they've been sitting. I don't know at what point in their life cycle they were picked or what was used to ripen them. I don't know if they have been exposed to pesticides and toxins. It surprised me to learn that many flowers purchased at florists or in the grocery store have been flown in from other countries and are loaded with toxic chemicals. I don't want to bring that into my home, and I don't want to support that type of growing in other communities. I want to provide those around me with healthy, wholesome options for food and flowers that they can trust as much as I do.

CREATIVE EXPRESSION

Creativity makes me feel alive, especially when working with nature's living canvas. A garden is an infinite art project that changes with each season, and I love to experiment with plant colors, various flowers, textures, and planting arrangements. There is so much to learn and so much to design. Every year the canvas changes, and that is incredibly exciting to me. This is my art and with flowers, more is more! It is so gratifying, and it is never finished, which is the best part.

PHYSICAL & MENTAL WELLNESS

Physical and mental wellness have become extremely important to me over the last few years. They are at the very top of my life goals. I am constantly striving to be the best version of me that I can be, and the garden oozes wellness in abundance. I want to soak up as much of it as possible. Not only does the garden provide nutritious produce that feeds and sustains my body, but working the land every day requires daily movement, exercise, sunshine, fresh air, and a connection with nature. We all need more of these things. Gardens clear the mind and smell like heaven. If you've tended to a garden, I'm sure you know what I'm talking about when I say that there have been many days where I go into the garden upset about something and come out of it feeling completely happy. The garden keeps me firmly rooted, stable, and at peace.

RESILIENCE & PATIENCE

Gardening has taught me how to fail, and then how to get back up again and keep trying until I find success. For example, when a crop does not thrive, I've learned to examine what I've done wrong, and then figure out a better plan for next year. I've learned that getting upset and giving up is not the answer. Failing can be a good thing if it teaches us important lessons. Having patience, positivity, and faith in the garden has been my path to success. I now find myself applying the same methods to other situations in life. It reminds me of a great quote by Yung Pueblo: "The mind is a garden; what we decide to grow there will determine our prosperity." If we can manage our minds right, we can do anything, and the same goes for our gardens.

I used to be a very impatient person, but in the garden, most of the work I do requires me to wait for my reward. Some plants take a few years to establish, and this means doing the work now and then being patient for the payoff, which has proven to be so worth it! This little lesson—which has proven time and time again that it isn't really little at all—has changed the way I feel about many things in life.

FINDING PURPOSE & MEANING

Being able to grow nutritious food and beautiful flowers for my family and for our community has given me a sense of purpose, for which I am eternally grateful. I feel that I am living a life aligned with my values, and with that comes a great deal of satisfaction and even confidence, which has been unexpected. Every day I wake up feeling a bit more sure of myself and why I am on this earth.

A SHIFT IN VALUES

What follows is the most important way gardening has changed my life. I used to think I'd find happiness by filling my days with things that gave me an instant reward. Things such as shopping, drinking alcohol, or eating junk food, which were exciting and had made me believe that the more of them I had, the happier I'd be. However, the garden has taught me that those things actually don't contribute to my happiness—and, in fact, they are thieves of joy. They are just exciting distractions that feel good in the moment but push me farther away from my life goals in the long run.

I've found success in the garden, which I view as the opposite of an instant reward. It's a daily routine where I have to be patient and build my dreams in a rested, healthy, and peaceful state of mind. This lesson is huge and can apply to my entire life. The garden has taught me that real joy and satisfaction come from taking action, making progress toward your goals each day, and from bypassing the empty distractions as much as possible. I can even go so far as to say that gardening brings me so much happiness that I am no longer tempted by the bad habits I used to struggle with. It's all about caring for ourselves the same way we nurture and care for the garden—little steps each day can eventually produce astounding results.

Gardening has taught me to seek out inner peace over excitement, long-term health and wellness over short-term fun and instant gratification, and true meaning over personal pleasure. It has shown me that helping others is what makes me feel useful, alive, and purposeful.

QUALITY TIME SPENT WITH FRIENDS & FAMILY

Working in the garden is fun for all ages. Having a serene, beautiful space to enjoy with the company of others is wonderful, especially when you helped create it. Whenever my girlfriends come over, we cut flowers and make bouquets as we catch up on our busy lives and swap stories. When family comes over, we cook with fresh ingredients from the garden and enjoy our meals and togetherness surrounded by cheery flowers and the sound of a trickling fountain. I will never tire of these moments, and the garden serves as the perfect backdrop.

SHARING WHAT I'VE LEARNED

After everything I have learned in the garden and around our farm, here is what I wish for you: I hope that these chapters and this story have given you the confidence to dive in, get your hands dirty, and grow something. If you've never planted a seed, do it! I assure you, it will teach you something valuable. If you've never cared for an animal, give it a try. It will bring you more joy than you think possible and grow your heart in ways you'd never expect. If you feel called to give, don't hesitate! I promise it will bring you satisfaction, fulfillment, and confidence. Reach out to those around you and share your passion. You will find yourself surrounded by genuine friends with shared values.

Find a way to plant a garden—whether it's planting pots of herbs on a windowsill, participating in a community plot, or running a whole farm—and receive the gifts that it brings. It will change your life just like it has changed mine.

Acknowledgments

Creating this book and sharing it with all of you has been a dream of mine for so long, and I would not have been able to do it without the help and encouragement from so many wonderful people in my life.

To my husband, Tom, none of this would exist without your tremendous support and hard work. Thank you for being the reliable, responsible, and generous husband that you are. Thank you for always standing behind my numerous big goals and plans—from starting a farm to building a massive garden to writing this book. Thank you for being so understanding and never complaining about my long hours, and for repeatedly picking up my slack around the house amid all the writing and photographing that went into *Blooms & Dreams*.

To my daughters, Leila and Lili, I am incredibly grateful to have been blessed with such fun and caring girls. Thank you for going on this beautiful journey with me, for helping out in the garden and around the farm—even at times when you didn't feel like it—and for putting up with a very busy mama. Thank you for helping me shoot some of the images for this book, and for occasionally letting me sneak an image with you in it.

To my uncle Eric Myers (Myers Literary Management), I can't thank you enough for volunteering your time and expert advice on all the correspondence and contracts needed to set this book deal into place. You have been beyond gracious and helpful, and it means the world to me.

Camilla Dugonjic, your insight has been invaluable. You are a true friend, and I thank you from the bottom of my heart. You're always willing to offer up honest and helpful feedback, even when you've just had a baby and moved across the world. Thank you for taking the time out of your busy schedule to read and reread what I've written.

Alexis Gonzalez, you are a gem. You're always available to assist in any capacity necessary. You have helped immensely in the garden, as well as with all my projects, and you do everything with such a kind demeanor and a smile on your face. I am incredibly grateful for you.

Helen Noren, I am ecstatic that our shared love of flowers has brought us together. Thank you for your countless trips out to the farm to help me harvest for the food bank, style and arrange photos for the book, film for my show, and work in the garden. You're always happy to roll up your sleeves and jump into whatever project I've got going on. Your open mind, creativity, kindness, and ability to love your friends so fiercely inspires me every single day.

Heidi Stephens, thank you for your continued efforts helping with the cutting, arranging, and donating of all the flowers and produce, for pulling weeds and working in the garden, and for always being willing to do fun photo shoots together with our bounties, despite being a very busy working mom. You are the voice of calm in my life and one the best neighbors, friends, and confidants a gal could hope for.

To the whole Larios family, your cheery attitude and work ethic are inspiring. Thank you for your endless assistance around the farm. Without you, none of this would be possible. To the entire Gibbs Smith team, thank you for believing in me, for being so uplifting and supportive, for helping me spread my message, and for being such a joy to work with. You've made my dreams come true!

Finally, thank you to my sisters, Krishni, Nila, and Heather, as well as my mom, for being such encouraging beacons of light in my life.

And, of course, thank you to all of you who are reading this book.